SEEKING PEACE
THROUGH RECONCILIATION

OVERCOMING RESISTANCE
WITHIN OURSELVES AND OTHERS

A GROUP STUDY
PART 2

DONALD E. JONES, PHD

J & A BOOK PUBLISHERS
www.jabookpublishers.com

ISBN-10:1-946368-04-0
ISBN-13:978-1-946368-04-1

DEDICATION

I dedicate this book to my Savior and Lord Jesus Christ. He has been with me every step of my journey upon the earth, and I so look forward to being in His presence forever and ever.

CONTENTS

CONTENTS

ACKNOWLEDGMENTS

I want to thank my wonderful and gracious wife Carol who has supported me in this ministry with sacrifice, enthusiasm, encouragement, and accountability. Most of all, she has been a constant blessing because of her willingness to listen. I was always sharing with her the truths God had been teaching me as I studied His word and wrote this book. It consumed many hours. Thank you, Carol, and I deeply love you.

I want to thank my son Gregory R. Jones for volunteering to be the primary editor of this important book. Without his time and effort in painstakingly and meticulously going over every word and every sentence checking and rechecking the sentence structure and grammar, I would not have been able to complete it. Thank you for your ministry to me. I love you my son.

I want to thank my other children, Krista, Matt, and Kara for their love for Christ and His Word and their willingness to live for Him. I love you all.

Introduction

This series of two books (Part 1,2) grew out of a desire to put the material in my main book on seeking peace through reconciliation into a format for group study. As a result, the introductions are exactly the same in both of the books. This is primarily due to the essential nature of the content to aid in our understanding of the truths found in each one. It also allows the books to be read and studied one after the other or to be studied independent of the other one. This provides more flexibility to the various individuals, groups, churches, and organizations who wish to use it.

In Matthew 14, after the feeding of the 5,000, Jesus sent His disciples by boat across the Jordan giving Himself time to disperse the crowd and find a place to pray alone. About the fourth watch of the night (3:00am - 6:00am), the boat was being battered by waves from a strong wind, and Jesus was seen by His disciples walking on the water. At first, they thought it was an apparition and screamed in fear, "It's a ghost!" Then Jesus cried out for them not to be afraid and identified Himself. Then in verse 28-29, the apostle records, "Peter answered him and said, 'Lord, if it is you, command me to come to you on the waters.' He said, 'Come!'"

So, Peter got out of the boat, walked on the water, and headed toward Jesus. Then he looked up and saw the great wind all around him. His eyes turned toward the sea, and he saw the powerful waves. Even in the presence of the Son of God, He became frightened and began to sink. He cried out for Jesus to save him. The Lord responded by immediately stretching out His hand and taking hold of him. Though the Lord could have said many things, he simply asked Peter, You of little faith why do you doubt?" Jesus walked Peter on the water to the safety of the boat. All became calm.

1

Often, we are like Peter in our relationship with Jesus. We love the Lord, and yet make mistakes, misunderstand His words and actions, and even fail to trust Him. We let the winds and torrents of our lusts and desires to get in the way of our devotion to Him. We allow the stormy seas of trouble and tribulation to make us doubt His intentions and power. We allow the flowing waters and winds of our busy lives to make us treat Jesus as an apparition and not a real person. Yet, regardless of how far we have sunk in our stupidity, weaknesses, and rebellious sin, He always reaches His hand out to restore the relationship we have with Him. The Lord Jesus is always willing to accept our struggles, tolerate our weaknesses, and forgive our sin. He is constantly reaching out to make peace with us. At every turn, Jesus, our Father God, and His Father, and the Spirit are ready to reconcile and restore the conflicts we bring into our relationship with Him.

Here is the point of mentioning this story. God desires the same out of all His children. This is found in several critical passages in the Holy Scriptures. Two of them are mentioned by our Lord and one from the apostle Paul. All three clearly explain the truth that relationships are to be "reconciled" and "restored" to "gain back" our brother, sister, or neighbor. This is done by seeking peace through reconciliation. We should constantly seek to resolve our conflicts with people.

In Matthew 5, the Lord Jesus discusses the heart attitudes people in God's kingdom should possess. After speaking of anger, the Lord presents a general principle of living in His kingdom on earth. In verses 23-24, He explains, "If therefore you are offering your gift at the altar, and there remember that your brother has anything against you, leave your gift there before the altar, and go your way. First be reconciled to your brother, and then come and offer your gift." The Greek word translated "reconciled" means "to make changes." It originates from a Greek root word that was a banking term meaning "to render accounts the same." There would be a discrepancy between two bank ledgers, and all the mistakes would have to be found and corrected in order for them to agree. We express this between people as "being on the same page." The Lord indicates that the Father desires His people to come to Him fully reconciled with each other. If we, as Christians, know that someone harbors something against us, we are to take the initiative and go to them and reconcile with them. We should not wait for them to come to us. We take our responsibility and go to them. We must once again "settle accounts." They have the same responsibility.

In Matthew 18, Jesus discusses those who are sinning in the church and what all believers should do. In verse 15, the Lord commands, "If your brother sins against you, go, show him his fault between you and him alone. If he listens to you, you have gained back your brother." The Greek word translated "gain" refers "to obtaining or securing something." When a relationship is restored, we gain back everything that the other parties contributed. In this particular case, we have something against our brother, rather than the reverse. If this does happen, we are to take the initiative and confront our brother or sister to gain him or her back and restore the relationship. So, whether someone has something against us, or we have something against someone else, the procedure is essentially the same. Christians must take the initiative and reconcile with them.

The third passage involves the restoration of a sinning brother in the church. In Galatians 6, Paul opens the chapter with an explanation of how to help a sinning saint. In verse one, Paul asserts, "Brothers, even if a man is caught in some fault, you who are spiritual must restore such a one." The Greek word translated "restore" means "to render fit, sound, or complete; to mend or repair what has been broken." The word is used of a physically broken fishing net. In Mark 1:19 and Matthew 4:21, when Jesus called James and John into ministry with Him, they were in the process of "mending" their fishing nets. They were mending the holes in their net so the fish would not fall through. This restoration could easily involve a conflict between two people. Holes in their relationship need to be mended. This process involves the seeking of peace with others. Keep them in mind.

These two books are original works on reconciliation and resolving conflicts. It is not based on other books that I have read and simply collated. To produce this work, I carefully read through the entire New Testament verse by verse and meticulously perused the Old Testament paying particular attention to the Psalms and Proverbs. As I read, categories were built from the individual passages, rather than a set of preconceived notions. These numerous categories became the individual biblical principles found in each chapter. Every passage was studied in its historical, grammatical, and scriptural contexts. Then, I compared all my interpretations with those of past and present scholars. After this study, I have attempted to obey and follow these biblical principles in my own personal life and also utilize them in my pastoral counseling practice. I have seen the Holy Spirit use them to transform relationships of all kinds.

One last thought. At the end of each chapter, I discuss a counseling experience. Due to confidentiality, none of these are based on one particular counseling situation. Instead, I have mixed together common elements I have seen, details from books and films, bits from my own life and the lives of people I have known, and thoughts from my imagination to create a situation where the biblical principles discussed in the chapters can fully be applied. These are composites of real-life situations. Read, learn, and apply.

Chapter 1

Refuse and Suffer

There may be a time in our lives where we simply refuse to reconcile with others (see Introduction). We might still be angry and bitter about what they did to us or our loved ones and decide, regardless of what the Scriptures say, we will not do it. We will not forgive them. We will not cover over their sins in love or go to a decision-making process. When this occurs, our Father, as a loving Father, steps in and trains us to follow His blueprint. The Lord Almighty will not allow His children to be in a state of constant conflict and strife. If we, as Christians, refuse to reconcile our relationships with others, then we, as God's children, could suffer the discipline and consequences of the Lord.

A Typical Scenario

Perhaps, you have had or heard a conversation between a grown child and his or her father that went something like this? The phone is answered and you say or hear, "Hello? Hi, dad what's up? (The dad responds.) What do you mean you can't make Natalie's recital? She is your only granddaughter! Since you missed all my activities, don't you think that you could make my daughter's recital? (The dad responds.) Oh, I understand alright! Well, I refuse to understand! I have spent my whole life hearing all your excuses. I could have written a book listing them all in detail. There have been so many over the years. Look Father, we are finished! You will never come to another event that involves Natalie. In fact, you will be lucky if you ever see her or even me again! Good bye for good and do not ever call me or my family ever!"

Sometimes, people will cause us to become angry, bitter, or upset as in this scenario. This might result in our refusal to resolve a problem. Rather than deal with an issue and reconcile a relationship, we shun, rebuff, gossip, backbite, or even cut the person off altogether. Unfortunately, this may also discontinue all the relationships that may be connected to that one, such as Natalie, who was the granddaughter in our scenario. She did nothing wrong and now cannot see her grandfather again. This may affect generations to come.

A Scriptural Principle

In this chapter we discuss a principle that deals with the many consequences that proceed from a refusal to reconcile a relationship. Before we decide to end or refuse to restore a relationship (see Introduction), we must understand the ramifications of this decision to us and others. Principle one is this, "if we refuse to reconcile, we will suffer the adverse consequences." Now, not all commands can be immediately obeyed, sometimes there may be a real struggle deep within our hearts to follow God. Why? To restore a relationship is truly a divine act, not a human one. To act divinely requires supernatural divine thinking and divine power. Our broken relationships must be viewed divinely to act differently.

A Biblical Explanation

Why would God make His children suffer if we will not reconcile with others? Why is getting along with people so important to Him? The answer is found in His own divine character. We cannot refuse to reconcile relationships with all people because our God is a God of peace (2 Corinthians 13:11; Romans 15:33). Therefore, His divine blueprint for relationships is the establishment of peace among people. He

6

desires peace between Himself and others. He desires peace among His children and between His children and the world (those who are unsaved). When the angels appeared to the shepherds, they began to sing, "Glory to God in the highest, on earth peace, good will toward men." These powerful angelic hosts were proclaiming that the peacemaker between God and man had been born (Luke 2:14).

Jesus, who is the exact image of the Father (Hebrews 1:3), is called the Prince of Peace (Isaiah 9:6). The Holy Spirit of God brings peace as one of His fruits for being filled with Him (Galatians 5:22). In Mark 9:50, Jesus, the Prince of Peace, declared, "Be at peace with one another." If believers refuse to reconcile, conflict occurs, not peace. In Hebrews 12:14, the author says, "Follow after peace with all men." Then in 1 Corinthians 13:11, Paul asserts that we are to "live in peace." In 1 Thessalonians 5:13, the apostle Paul clearly states, "Be at peace among yourselves." This is what the Lord desires in our interactions with others. When God's people refuse to follow His blueprint of peace found only in reconciliation, God might intervene, and there could be consequences.

The first consequence is direct discipline from God. As we live our Christian lives on earth, we should grow more and more like our Father in heaven and into the image of His Son Jesus Christ through the power of the Spirit. In 2 Corinthians 3:18, the apostle Paul explained that all Christians are being "transformed into the same image from glory to glory, even as from the Lord, the Spirit." Christlikeness is the goal of our Christian lives. In fact, the purpose of the Lord's church is to conform all believers "to the stature of the fullness of Christ" (Ephesians 4:13).

When we are unwilling to conform to Christ's stature in reconciliation and restoration of relationships, our Father will provide some assistance through His discipline and training process. If we will not be at peace, as our God is at peace, then He will compel us as His children through His discipline. This is taught in Hebrews 12:4-11. God as a loving Father disciplines His children to be righteous just like a human father does. A father spends time teaching his kids to get along and work things out among themselves and with their siblings. This is the sharing and peace process that is a fundamental practice parents teach their children.

The second consequence for refusing to reconcile might come from the local church where the believers attend. Not only can the Lord intervene directly, but He can also work through His church. In Matthew 18:15, we are told what should be done if someone has sinned against us. We must go and gently confront them. If they listen to us, we have gained back our brother. Then in verse 16, the Lord states, "But if he doesn't listen, take one or two more with you, that at the mouth of two or three witnesses every word may be established." These witnesses are not just people that we told about the offense but people who had witnessed the offense themselves. In our context, it would those who had seen the actual incident or perhaps had seen bitter, angry, or hateful words and actions done by the one to the other. This would also be a perfect time to affirm many of the actual facts to the offending party.

They would also witness the repentance or unwillingness to repent of the offender. This keeps the actual problem from becoming a deadlock on who said what. The case might arise where the person who thinks he bears no responsibility actually does, and he may also have to repent. The witnesses may attempt to mediate the situation themselves, find a mediator for the parties, or request the two parties to search for one themselves. If the person or possibly both still refuse to repent and reconcile, these witnesses should approach the elders of the church they attend.

The church would listen to the testimony of the witnesses to ascertain the facts as the final judge in the matter. They must be certain concerning the facts. The church leadership may decide to speak to the offender if they have questions about the situation. The leaders may desire to interview all others involved. The church leaders might desire to mediate the situation themselves, find a mediator for the parties, or require the two parties to search for one themselves. They should give the offender an opportunity to repent.

Once the church has determined that there is unrepentant sin occurring, they will begin the final step of discipline. It is important to note that physical words and actions are the only things that can be dealt with. The church cannot look into the hearts of people, but believers are required to love the brethren (John 13:34), the unsaved (Romans 13:8), and even our enemies (Matthew 5:44). These do not refer to our inward feelings but our outward words and actions (1 John 3:18). When we refuse to reconcile and it issues forth in sinful words or actions, this can be disciplined.

It's important to note that people cannot be forced to have a "relationship" with a particular person; they choose to have one. Jesus had an acquaintance relationship with those He taught (Matthew 4:23-24), a "disciple" relationship with the twelve (Matthew 10:1), a "friendship" with three (Matthew 17:1), and a "deep friendship" with one (John 21:7). The Bible does not say we have to have an equal closeness to every believer. We are able to pick and choose, but we must still love them and not hate them in words and actions. If we decide not to engage in a relationship with someone, this is fine. We cannot be forced, but we may not hate them in words and actions. The only exception is marriage. One may not simply decide to end a marriage for any reason (though many do) and then find another one (1 Corinthians 7:10-11). This is not acceptable to the Lord God.

In Matthew 18:17, the Lord Jesus continues, "If he refuses to listen to them, tell it to the assembly." Here we lay out all the details and allow the church to encourage the brothers or sisters to repent and reconcile. If they refuse to listen to the church and repent, Jesus commands, "Let him be to you as a Gentile or a tax collector." The Lord is speaking to the Jews. The term Gentiles refer to those outside the faith. We treat them solely as unbelievers.

History tells us that the tax-collectors collaborated with the Romans to collect taxes. They charged huge amounts for their services and gouged the Jews. They were considered not only unbelievers but the worst of them. Jesus explains that Christians who refuse to repent of their sins after having gone through this three-step process should be treated as unbelievers of the worst kind. Basically, if they desire to act like unbelievers, then they should be treated as such. This means we are to disassociate ourselves from the person until the time that they repent and reconcile with us.

The third consequence or act of suffering may come from the government if we have broken any laws (violence, abuse, etc.) or need legal assistance (separation, divorce, etc.). The apostles clearly describe the government as an instrument of God. It was placed into power by the Lord and may become involved if the conflict escalates or it cannot be resolved.

In 1 Peter 2:13-14, the apostle Peter writes, "Therefore subject yourselves to every ordinance of man for the Lord's sake: whether to the king, as supreme; or to governors, as sent by him." We are to submit to the governing authorities. Why? Peter continues, "For vengeance on evildoers and for praise to those who do well." They are to punish wickedness and evil and praise goodness. If we refuse to reconcile and the conflict then intensifies, it could lead to breaking the law. Then, the government may intervene.

This is not the only responsibility of the government, in Romans 13:4, Paul asserts, "For he is a servant of God to you for good. But if you do that which is evil, be afraid, for he doesn't bear the sword in vain; for he is a servant of God, an avenger for wrath to him who does evil." Paul explains that the police and other officials are to bring fear into people's hearts to prevent them from escalating the strife into horrific words and actions. This also may prompt reconciliation. It certainly may protect the parties from taking actions they will regret. Another responsibility is to be a peace keeping force in the world. Paul wrote to Timothy to not only pray for the salvation of all government officials but to pray that they would allow Christians to "lead a tranquil and quiet life in all godliness and reverence" (1 Timothy 2:2). Implied in this injunction is this peace keeping concept.

The people cannot live peaceful and quiet lives unless the government takes on this important responsibility. To pray for peace for Christians by necessity implies they are able and desirous of keeping the peace in the first place. All of the laws instituted to govern contracts, property, divorce, and custody, to name a few, are created to keep the peace. If we refuse to reconcile and it leads to disrupting the peace, then suffering at the hands of the government may come.

The fourth consequence that may occur when we refuse to restore a relationship might be the terrible inner anguish that comes from a broken heart, anger, bitterness, despair, fear, or grief. The destruction of a relationship might bring some or all of these emotions and many others. After King David sinned with Bathsheba, he attempted to hide it until Nathan exposed him. It was this occasion that caused David to write Psalm 51 and reflect upon the anguish he felt when he refused to reconcile with God. It was this moment of repentance and restoration of his deep relationship with God that brought a wonderful sense of relief from the pain and suffering he felt. The inner anguish was replaced with great joy. Later, David will concern himself with the restoration of all other relationships involved in his sin.

In Psalm 51:8, David describes his emotional pain as "The bones which you have broken." The torment was so difficult and intense that it felt like all his bones in his body had been broken. He was immobilized in misery. In Psalm 32, which must have been a similar occasion, this repentant king David compared the inner torture from his transgressions with the inner agony of a physical crushing of the body. In Psalm 32:3, he remembered, "When I kept silence, my bones wasted away through my groaning all day long." Refusing to repent of his sin caused a deep groaning within him as if his very bones were wasting away inside his frail body. In verse 4, he continues, "For day and night your hand was heavy on me." He depicts God as pressing His divine hand upon him day and night until it was too great to bear.

He finishes the verse with "My strength was sapped in the heat of summer." God's divine hand weighed so heavily upon him that it sapped him of strength in the same way the sun does in the heat of summer. Jerusalem can easily go to triple digits. This might cause someone to become feeble and debilitated. Our suffering can also go to the triple digit mark as it widens and deepens when someone refuses to mend a broken relationship with us.

Next, the fifth consequence for refusing to reconcile may be the terrible heartache of watching the pain and suffering brought to the innocent individuals, especially children, who may love the person, who is despised and hated. We must know that inside all of us are many generations who might suffer terribly for our angry, bitter choices. We may have to come to grips with this distinct possibility in order to find the motivation to reconcile.

An Ancient Portrait

The Old Testament provides an enlightening example of bitterness, anger, and grudge bearing that led eventually to violence between two half-brothers and a sister. In 2 Samuel 13 the story is told of Absalom, Amnon, and Tamar. King David had several wives who had children. Absalom, one of David's sons, had a beautiful sister named Tamar. Amnon, one of Absalom's half-brothers, fell in love with her. In fact, Amnon was so in love and in lust with her that he became frustrated and made himself ill. He wanted to sleep with her, but she was a virgin and desired to keep the marriage bed sacred. Amnon had a sneaky, crafty, conniving cousin who decided to help him in his lustful frustration. His name was Jonadab. He asked his cousin, addressing him as "O Son of the King," why he looked so depressed. Amnon told him that he was disheartened because he wanted his half-sister, Tamar. So Jonadab conjured up a plan to solve the problem.

He suggested that this son of the king pretend to be sick and when his father, David, came to visit him, he should ask if Tamar could bring him some food to eat. Perhaps, she could even prepare it right in front of him, so Amnon might watch. Then as his sweet, naive sister served and comforted him in his affliction, Amnon would take her. This was forbidden by God. In Leviticus 11:9, He says, "You shall not uncover the nakedness of your sister, the daughter of your father, or the daughter of your mother, whether born at home, or born abroad."

Then in Leviticus 18:11 God also states, "You shall not uncover the nakedness of your father's wife's daughter, conceived by your father, since she is your sister." Later in Deuteronomy 27:22, Moses reiterates this commandment, "Cursed is he who lies with his sister, his father's daughter or his mother's daughter. All the people shall say, 'Amen.'"

They knew his suggestion was a sin. Yet, Amnon put the plan into action. David, who should have been much more discerning, bought the whole act and summoned his sister Tamar. According to the customs at the time, any unmarried daughter was usually kept in seclusion from men so that no one could see them alone and be tempted. David did not follow this custom and asked her to make some cakes in Amnon's presence and feed her brother to assist him in his weakened state. She [Tamar] did not protest at all because she trusted her half-brother to respect her virginity.

When Amnon feigned his sickness, Tamar came to serve him. Perhaps, she thought that she was his angel of mercy; instead, she was about to become a victim of rape. So, Tamar traveled to Amnon's house. In front of him, she took the dough, then kneaded it, and made cakes for him. Amnon watched her prepare the cakes while burning with desire for her. Finally, when the whole process was over, she set the cakes before him, innocently expecting him to eat.

Immediately, Amnon refused to eat, and he sent everyone out of the house. Then, he told her to bring the food into the bedroom and asked her to feed him from her hand while he lied down. When she reached over to him with the cake, he grabbed her hand and demanded, "My sister, come, lie with me." He addressed her as a sibling, rather than as a woman. This demonstrated the extent of his evil perversion. Tamar refused and begged him not to violate her.

She begged and begged him not to take away her most valued possession. This would be disgraceful in the nation of Israel. Amnon would be disgraced because he had raped her. His sister would be disgraced because she would lose her virginity and would be considered unholy and defiled. Their family would be disgraced because this shameful thing was never ever done. Tamar explained that she would never rid herself of this humiliating reputation, and Amnon would be considered a complete fool among his people. She implored him to simply speak to their father, and he would let them marry properly. However, as lust filled his heart and body, he refused to wait. Since he was much stronger than her, he forced himself on her and violated her. Once the deed was done, his lustful, loving feelings immediately turned to disgust and hate for her. The author says that his hate was even greater than his love had been. When he was done with her, he screamed at her to get out! He was such a hypocrite that though he was the one who violated her against her will, he now saw her as defiled and dirty.

Then Tamar pleaded with Amnon to let her stay, sending her away was even worse than violating her. People would think that she had instigated this shameful act. She begged him to marry her and end this embarrassment. Since she would not leave, he had several of his servants throw her out and lock the door. How utterly humiliating! She was the daughter of the king of Israel. The virgin daughters of the king would wear long-sleeved garments to signify their virginity and wholesomeness. When this happened, she tore her long sleeves off and put ashes on her head. She put her hand on her head in shame and went away crying aloud in humiliation.

She went right into the arms of her brother Absalom. He knew right away what had happened. He asked her if she had been violated by Amnon. When she told him that she had, Absalom asked her to remain silent because he would handle it in his own way. Her brother explained that her silence would be the way to keep this terrible atrocity within the confines of their family. Obviously, he reasoned in his mind, "If a family member did the harm, then it would take another family member to get revenge." His sister remained "desolate" in Absalom's house the rest of her life. This meant she would never ever marry. What a tragedy! But the story continues. Eventually, her father, King David heard about what happened. The Scriptures indicate that he got angry. That's all. There was no fatherly discipline or even any legal ramifications for this horrendous act. Nothing! After this, Absalom hated his half-brother and did not speak to Amnon for two years. For two years he let the bitterness well up inside him, until finally the moment of revenge came.

It was the time of the year when the sheep were sheared, and the owners of the sheep would have a feast. So Absalom invited all his half-brothers (the sons of the king) to a sheep shearing feast. First, he invited his father and all his servants, knowing his father David would refuse to come. Yet, he kept insisting which would soften David's heart toward his plight of not being able to celebrate with his family members. In this way, his real plan could go into effect. So, he asked his father if he could invite all his brothers (blood and half). He wanted Amnon but the pretense required all his brothers. He specifically mentioned Amnon's name.

King David was not the least bit suspicious, even though Absalom had not spoken to Amnon in two years. Did David not know that? Nevertheless, David agreed and blessed him. Then, Absalom left. As soon as he arrived home, Absalom commanded his servants to strike Amnon when he became drunk at the celebration. Though they protested, He told them not to be fearful, even though they were striking the king's son. He would simply say they were obeying him. He desired all the revenge and would take all the blame. He encouraged them to be bold and courageous as they killed him! So, his servants prepared themselves. During the party, Amnon became intoxicated, and they murdered him.

Then their other brothers immediately fled. So, Absalom killed his brother through others, as his own father David killed Uriah through others. When the other brothers were on the road home, David falsely received word that all of his sons had been killed by Absalom. He tore his garments and lay upon the ground in mourning. Of course, Absalom had to flee. When David's watchman saw the other sons coming, he informed David. When they were all reunited, the king and his sons wept bitterly for Amnon.

Absalom headed to his other family for safety. He found protection with Talmia the son of Ammihud, his maternal grandfather, who was the king of Geshur (2 Samuel 3:3). According to Numbers 35:21, Absalom deserved the death penalty for pre-meditated murder. As a result, he needed the protection of a king and army. David mourned for his son every day.

Absalom stayed there for over three years. David's heart was broken over Absalom and was comforted concerning Amnon because he was already dead. What happened next was a terrible tragedy. Absalom was so angry because David refused to see him, the son took over the realm from his father! He literally ran David out of his kingdom. David was heartsick as he fled for his life.

The point is that Amnon did a despicable and horrifying evil deserving the full weight of the law on his shoulders. Yet, Absalom was not the law. Absalom refused to reconcile with him and let his jealousy and anger churn for two long years while he bore a bitter grudge and spent much time plotting his revenge on his half-brother.

What a terrible situation everyone was in. The ultimate result was the division of David's family, David losing his kingdom to Absalom, and then Amnon and Absalom losing their lives in death. We need to reconcile our relationships with others and not allow the flesh to become angry and bitter which causes multiple problems for ourselves and the others. We cannot refuse to reconcile. Even if it takes much time, we must reconcile.

A Modern Anecdote

Often times, a congregation of believers see their pastor upfront on Sunday mornings with a smile on his face and the joy of the Lord in his heart which is simply contagious. Yet, they are not immune from the disappointments of life and sometimes responding in a less than God honoring way. One such pastor came to my office to discuss his relationship with a fellow pastor in a city some fifty miles away. He was the pastor of a small church who was struggling with their finances and attendance and needed to make a dramatic move. His pastor friend had a large congregation and was well known, admired, and respected throughout the state. The pastor of the small church decided to ask his friend to come and do a weeklong series of messages on marriage which would attract a large crowd. The entire congregation was thrilled.

There were months of preparation. Almost everyone in the church became involved. A larger stage was planned and built by hand. The church band recruited members from nearby churches and practiced relentlessly. Many purchased and prepared large amounts of refreshments to serve the numerous guests. Brochures were carefully prepared, and gospel booklets purchased. When the offerings were not enough to cover the expenses, the church took out a small loan. As the day grew nearer, their anticipation grew. The church bought ads in the local paper, put up numerous flyers around their small town, and posted on as many social media sites as they could. It seemed as if their excitement was increasing by the minute.

A room was reserved for the pastor at the best hotel in town so he could have the privacy needed to prepare. The whole town was talking about the arrival of this famous pastor and the other pastor's church. The Wednesday before his Sunday arrival, the pastor cancelled. He sent his friend an email stating he had made too many other commitments and had to cut back. The small church pastor was completely devastated. Repeatedly, he attempted to contact his friend but to no avail. The church secretary told him that the pastor had traveled out of town, and he could not be reached. Unfortunately, the event had to be cancelled, and the people were broken-hearted. When he explained the cancelation at an emergency church meeting the next night, deep inside him came an anger and bitterness that he had never felt.

He could not understand how a friend, who was closer than a brother, could do such a thing. They had known each other since childhood, were best friends throughout school, played city league baseball, and attended the same college and seminary. In response to his feelings, he sent the ex-friend a scathing email. What they had in this temporal life on earth was over, but he would see him eternally in heaven.

He knew this was wrong, but he was so conflicted that he came to me for advice. I explained to him all the principles from the Scriptures in this book. I implored him to go and reconcile with his brother. With that, he stood up and said he would let me know. When he returned the following week, he was even more bitter and disturbed. The more he thought about it, the more he grew in his resolve not to restore this relationship. Once in a while, I may encounter a stubborn heart and then do my best to be understanding and gentle.

Yet, when we choose to disobey the very commands of the Father and decide to follow our own bitter hearts, I must issue a stern warning. So, I discussed with him the all the truths in this chapter and warned him that God disciplines His children. If he refused to follow God's holy mandate, he would suffer the consequences. Many weeks went by before I heard from him, while his anger and resultant bitterness had begun to affect all of his relationships. The church leaders were split on what to do with him. His wife was pulling away, and his children were wondering what was wrong with their dad. After three months, I received a call from the pastor. He thanked me for my advice from the Word and told me that he had decided to reconcile with his friend. All was well again.

A Personal Response

Dear Heavenly Father,

Lord, I realize I have been stubborn, angry, and bitter in my unwillingness to reconcile with (add name). I have really harbored a grudge for (list transgressions) against me. All along I had been suffering the consequences and still refused to restore the relationship. I have not thought of the others (list names) who had been affected by what my refusal has done to them. Father, I am so sorry. Please help me go to (add name) and restore the relationship. I pray in the name of Jesus. Amen.

Chapter 2

Love the Obstinate

Sometimes, no matter what we do to resolve the conflict, people choose to stand against us or end the relationship. What do we do then? We may see them at gatherings of friends or a family event, how do we treat them? When they refuse to reconcile and choose to be obstinate, we must love them anyway. Our response to their obstinacy is not based upon their response to us; instead, it is based upon God and what He desires. When we find ourselves suddenly in a conflict or stalemate, we can take our eyes off the Lord, and put them squarely upon the other person. This change in perspective almost certainly will lead to nothing but mutual retaliation making the problem worse. Whether they decide to reconcile with us or not, our God desires that we still love them through words and actions.

A Typical Scenario

Have you ever had or perhaps heard a conversation that a husband had with his wife concerning their daughter that went something like this: He says, "Hi Honey! Well, I called our daughter three times, and she won't answer. Her brother is getting married; you would think she would want to come to his wedding? This is all messed up. This estrangement is going to tear the family apart. If she keeps this up, she will never meet her sister-in-law or see many of her future nieces and nephews. (Wife responds.) What? Exactly, we won't be able to go to her wedding, meet our son-in-law, and ever see our future grandchildren. Doesn't she realize this is going to affect generations of our families and all the other families involved for many years to come? What? (Wife responds.) Yes, I have tried everything to reconcile. She simply won't respond. It has been five years already! There is nothing else I can do!" Here the father has taken all the right steps to reconcile with his daughter, but she will not respond.

A Scriptural Principle

In a perfect world, when we have proceeded through the steps we have discussed so far, the relationship is restored. All is well with the world. Most of the time, in our imperfect world, the relationship is still restored. At other times, it is not. Sometimes people become obstinate and are unwilling to restore the relationship. In this chapter, we will study how we are to exactly respond to them. If they choose to be bitter, angry, or bear a grudge, what do we do? If they decide to hate, criticize, or even get revenge, how do we react? If the relationship is not only ended but they begin acting like a bitter enemy, how should we respond to them? The answer is found in the next Scriptural principle. Principle two is "if someone refuses to reconcile, we must love them anyway."

A Biblical Explanation

When people refuse to reconcile with us, our flesh wants to respond in like manner. It is called "retaliation." If they hate us, we will hate them. If they ignore us, we will ignore them. If they criticize us, we will criticize them. If they take revenge, we will take revenge. Unfortunately, this leads to a spiral downward into every kind of evil. David asserts in Psalm 37:8 "Cease from anger and forsake wrath. Don't fret, it leads only to evildoing." Retaliation and revenge lead to utter devastation. It destroys relationships, ravages families, ruins friendships, and can split churches in half. This is not

God's way. Paul explains God's way in 1 Thessalonians 5:15, "See that no one returns evil for evil to anyone, but always follow after that which is good, for one another, and for all." So, when people harm us, we are not to seek their harm in return. Instead, we are to seek their good. In Romans 12:19-21, Paul reiterates this concept again, "Don't seek revenge yourselves, beloved, but give place to God's wrath. For it is written, 'Vengeance belongs to me; I will repay, says the Lord.' Therefore 'If your enemy is hungry, feed him. If he is thirsty, give him a drink; for in doing so, you will heap coals of fire on his head.' Don't be overcome by evil but overcome evil with good."

What if they break the law? In Romans 13:1-4, the apostle speaks of the governmental authorities as God's arm to avenge in a just way. We can notify the authorities, if they break the law. What if they attempt to physically hurt us? It is perfectly natural and human to defend ourselves whether it be in words or actions. The government, whether local or national, allows its citizens to hinder or stop an attack upon themselves by other citizens using both words and actions. The key in self-defense is to stop an attack, not then begin a new attack ourselves upon another. Though physical harm may occasionally happen, most of the time obstinacy entails verbal criticisms, the termination of a relationship, or even ignoring someone. What do we do?

The Lord Jesus provides the answer to their question in Matthew 5:43, when He discusses one of the beliefs of the Jews of His time. Jewish traditions claimed, "You shall love your neighbor and hate your enemy." The Jews of His time believed in retaliation. Instead, Jesus claims we are to love, bless, do good to, pray for, and not resist our enemies. Since they have chosen not to reconcile with us, then they have for all intents and purposes become our enemy. As a result, we should no longer pursue the relationship; instead, we should simply respond to them as they may have need. We become available if they ask for our help. We might even look for opportunities to meet their needs.

First, if given the chance, we should show them real love. Jesus states in Matthew 5:44 and Luke 6:27 that Christians are to love their enemies. The word "love" in this passage has nothing to do with romance but something much deeper. The Greek word essentially means to value or prize someone or something. This word was utilized by Jesus and His disciples to speak of valuing to the point of sacrifice. The classic use of the word is in John 3:16, where Jesus asserts that God so loved the world that He gave His Son. God so valued the world that He gave even though it was hostile to Him.

So, if they come to us with important needs to be met, we should value them and make the sacrifice. Though, we have two constraints on our love as Christians: we must love in knowledge and discernment. This means we are to know the situation fully and know the biblical principles that govern that situation; then, we must discern the best way to love the person. In Philippians 1:9, Paul declares, "This I pray, that your love may abound yet more and more in knowledge and all discernment." If we have an estranged family member who has a gambling problem, it would not be prudent to give them cash to meet their need.

Second, if given the chance, we should give a blessing to them. Not only are Christians to love their enemies but bless them. In the passages of Matthew 5:44 and Luke 6:28, we, as Christians, are commanded to bless those who curse them. Blessing someone was a very familiar Old Testament idea. A typical blessing is found in Ruth 2:3-5, when Boaz arrives at his fields and greets his reapers with "May the Lord be with you," and they return with "May the Lord bless you." This general blessing was full of meaning. These words expressed a genuine and heartfelt desire that the other person would find protection and safety in God. In Numbers 6:22-27, the Lord told Moses to have Aaron bless the people of Israel and present the words the Lord gave him to speak. He was to declare that the Lord bless them, keep them, make His face shine on them, be gracious to them, lift up His countenance on them, and give them peace. This was a manifold blessing for God to pour out His grace upon them.

This blessing is in contrast to cursing them. Paul speaks of this kind of blessing that should be made upon the enemies of Christians. In Romans 12:14, Paul commands, "Bless those who persecute you; bless, and don't curse." God's children should wish His blessing upon their persecutors or enemies, both in their hearts and from their mouths. Obviously, God's ultimate blessing would be in their own repentance from their evil responses to our attempts at reconciliation and the salvation of their souls.

Third, if given the chance, we should do good to them. Not only are Christians to love and bless their enemies, they are to "do good" to them. In Matthew 5:44 and Luke 6:27, believers are commanded by the Lord Jesus to do good to those who hate them. When believers are seeking to do good works for the glory of God, they must look to their enemies. In our case, those who are estranged can become recipients of our righteous deeds. In Matthew 5:16, the Lord Jesus proclaimed, "Even so, let your light shine before men; that they may see your good works, and glorify your Father who is in Heaven." We must let our lights shine before the world. When others refuse to reconcile with us, doing good shines our light toward them. This demonstrates that we are not like them; instead, we are like our Father. God continues to love us in spite of our sinful stubbornness toward Him. This is out of His grace and mercy.

In Ephesians 2:10, the apostle Paul describes Christians as God's workmanship, created in Christ Jesus for good works. He then encourages his readers to walk in them. One of our purposes upon this earth is to walk in good works. These good works most certainly extend to those who are obstinate and will not reconcile. In Galatians 6:9, the apostle exhorts his readers, "Let us not be weary in doing good, for we will reap in due season, if we don't give up." Then in verse 10, he declares, "So then, as we have opportunity, let's do what is good toward all men, and especially toward those who are of the household of the faith." Paul exhorted the Galatians to never ever give up doing good toward others whenever they have the opportunity. We need to heed these critical words when it comes to those who are obstinate. If an opportunity presents itself, we should seize it and meet their needs. This might build a bridge back to a relationship or at least it will honor our Father in heaven.

Fourth, we should pray for those who refuse to reconcile with us. In Matthew 5:44 and Luke 6:28, Christians are told to pray for those who mistreat them. What do we pray for? If they are unbelievers, we should pray for their salvation and God would help us restore the relationship with them. We should entreat the Lord to use our good deeds toward them to build a bridge or at least bring them to Christ. Paul and the other apostles witnessed numerous people receive Jesus as Savior and Lord who had previously opposed them. We should pray that God would open their eyes so they might become believers in Him and even proclaimers of the gospel.

In Acts 16, Paul was thrown into prison in Philippi. It can be reasonably assumed the jailor did not give him a warm reception, since he was ordered to put Paul and Silas into the stocks. Then in verses 35-41, Paul saved the jailor from killing himself after an earthquake split the jail open. The jailor knew that even if one prisoner escaped, he would be held responsible and killed. Paul stopped the jailor's rash suicide attempt indicating that all the prisoners remained in custody. This good work gave Paul the opportunity to share the gospel, and the jailor and his whole household received Christ as Savior and Lord. The jailer went from rejecting the gospel to accepting Christ and becoming one of the original members of the newly founded church at Philippi.

In Acts 18:1-11, Paul preached the gospel and was thrown out of the synagogue in Corinth. The apostle then set himself up in the house of Titius Justus next door and continued preaching the good news. Eventually Crispus, the leader of the synagogue, with all His household came to Christ. This enemy of Paul and his gospel became a friend and advocate of the gospel. This happened numerous times in the ministry of Paul: previous enemies became followers and friends.

If those estranged to us are believers, then we should pray that God would open their hearts to us. We should ask God to convict them of their stubbornness in not being willing to reconcile. In Ephesians chapter 6, Paul commands the saints to put on the full armor of God. Then in verse 18, he finishes his discussion with a powerful exhortation to watch and pray for believers who are in the battle. He writes, "With all prayer and requests, praying at all times in the Spirit, and being watchful to this end in all perseverance and requests for all the saints."

Would not the battle against the forces of evil entail our sinning against others and their unwillingness to reconcile? Would it not encompass their sinning against us and their unwillingness to repent? Both of these require a battle, and both may require much prayer not only by other believers but the one who desires to reconcile for the other who does not. Believers need the Lord God's power to move the hearts of people. This is accomplished supernaturally in prayer.

Fifth, if given the chance, we should be unwilling to resist them in time of need; instead, we should go out of our way to meet them. In Matthew 5:39-41 and Luke 6:29-30, the Lord Jesus declared that His followers should not resist their enemies. The Greek word which is translated "resist" means "to oppose or stand against." A careful reading of the context demonstrates that it involves dealing with enemies in need. In Matthew 5:42, after giving three examples of not resisting enemies, Jesus proclaimed a truth or principle to guide our interactions with people in general and especially those who oppose us. We are to give to anyone who asks or wants to borrow from us. We are to act like our Lord God who sends sunshine and rain upon evil as well as good people. We can never forget this!

Christians will go out of their way, beyond their comfort zone to meet the needs of people, even the obstinate or their enemies. Do others need something believers have and then humiliate them to get it? There is no need to challenge them, the obstinate can have it. Do others sue believers because they need something those saints may be wearing? They do not need to bother, they will give two articles of clothing to these people, enemies or not. Do others need the saints to help them carry something a long distance? There will be no problem, they will be glad to carry it twice as far. As God's children, we are not like other people even our enemies will be helped. We will respond with love and allow our God to respond with justice.

An Ancient Portrait

A good illustration of this principle is found in the Old Testament. Though his uncle Laban deceived and cheated Jacob over and over, Jacob continually showed him love and respect. The story begins with Jacob fleeing from Esau to his uncle Laban's household. When Jacob arrived at a well, he met some men, and inquired as to whether they knew Laban or not. While Jacob was speaking, Rachel, who was one of Laban's two daughters and a shepherdess, approached the well to water her flock of sheep. It was love at first sight. The well had a large stone over it. So, he ran up, moved the stone, identified himself as a relative of her father Laban, and kissed her on the cheek. He was so overwhelmed by her that he began to weep. She ran and told her father. Once Laban heard the news, he ran out to greet Jacob and invited him in to stay. For a month, Jacob enjoyed his hospitality, until one day, his uncle Laban made a proposition.

He wanted to pay Jacob for the work that he was doing for him. Jacob immediately responded with his own offer. He desired only one wage, and it was the hand of Rachel in marriage. So, Jacob offered his uncle seven years of service for Rachel. Jacob was in love! Moses wrote that the seven years was as a few days because of his love for her. When the time finally came, Jacob came for his promised bride and consummated the marriage with his bride Rachel. By ancient custom, the bride would be veiled until the marriage was consummated. When morning came, Jacob discovered his uncle was really a treacherous man. He had replaced Rachel with his older daughter Leah. Since, the bride had remained veiled, Laban's trickery could be accomplished. When Jacob awoke, he confronted his uncle concerning this terrible deceit. He had worked seven years, as was their agreement, and he should have received Rachel as his only bride and wife. Unfortunately, in that culture the father had ultimate authority so Jacob could not just run away with her.

Laban's response was clear and direct. In his family, the older daughter was to be married off first. If Jacob would complete the marriage week with Leah, he could then have his permission to marry Rachel. Once he completed Rachel's marriage week, he had to work another seven years. As Jacob worked, his family grew. Eventually, Jacob had eleven sons and one daughter, and God told him it was time for him to return to his father's homeland. Laban insisted he stay and claimed that he had divined that it was the Lord's will. To convince him, his uncle offered him whatever wages he desired to stay. Jacob responded by explaining that all he had done for Laban had prospered, but he wasn't building a financial base for his own family. Laban was a shrewd man and knew he depended on Jacob's wisdom and relationship to God for his prosperity and kept insisting.

So, Jacob conceded and trusted his uncle once again. For his wages, Jacob would take all of Laban's speckled, spotted, and streaked sheep and goats to raise up his own flocks. In this way his flocks would be clearly distinguishable from Laban's. If any other sheep or goats were found among his flocks, his uncle Laban could consider them stolen. Then, the two agreed. Uncle Laban separated the designated animals from his own flocks and had his men drive them a journey of three days away. This way, Jacob's new flocks could not mate with the other ones. Laban thought Jacob would have to begin with such a small number that it would guarantee Jacob's service for years to come. Since Jacob was a believer and righteous man, he did not retaliate against his uncle. God had already told Jacob in a dream that he would bless all those animals.

As Laban saw God blessing Jacob's flocks, he decided to alter the terms of their arrangement ten different times. If the Lord God multiplied one kind of animal, Laban would take them. Then God would bless another kind. His uncle would return them and take the others. This happened over and over again. God kept blessing Jacob's flocks over Laban's. As a result, God had avenged Jacob, rather than him doing it on his own. The more obstinate Laban became, the more Jacob responded in love. After six short years, Jacob's flocks were enormous. This allowed him to add many servants, camels, and donkeys to his wealth. Once the sons of Laban, Jacob's cousins, saw what was happening, they became very jealous. Since Jacob's original flocks came from their father's flocks, they claimed that he had stolen the animals from their father and prospered off him. They ignored the fourteen years he had worked for their sisters. Once Jacob began to hear the grumblings, he decided it was time to depart or things could get rough. He determined not to notify Laban, so he could avoid his wrath. Once again, the Lord told Jacob to go back to his homeland, where God's promise of prosperity lied. The Lord God promised He would be with him all through his journey home.

When Laban found out, he pursued after Jacob and then confronted his nephew. The uncle refused to fully reconcile the way God would desire and instead asked for a treaty. He did not want a future war between their clans. Yet, Jacob loved him, in spite of this. Had Laban reconciled with Jacob in a holy way, their relationship could have been restored to perhaps an even greater level. Jacob made peace as best he could. Sometimes, this is all we are able to do as believers. So, if someone will not reconcile the relationship, we should at least love them on whatever level we can, even if they desire to be an enemy.

A Modern Anecdote

Friendships are often easy to begin but very difficult to end. We seem to know intuitively how to start a variety of relationships but seem to stumble around when we need to get out of one of them. When this happens, there sometimes can be horrible consequences. A woman named Joyce, who did not end a relationship well, made an appointment with me. She described herself as a happy, upbeat, and positive person. She did not like being around negative people ever. This made her happiness fade away and a kind of darkness come. This depressed her, so she avoided people like that. She had just broken up with a friend and told me the story. They were cashiers in a supermarket. It all started when a dog ran into the store. It was a little thing which obviously was hungry and had nowhere to go. The two of them chased the dog all over the store until she caught him. The other ran into the break room to get a paper bowl and took some food from her lunch, and they took it outside and fed him. They discovered that they were both dog lovers and were happy they had found someone with a common interest.

While the dog was feeding, they got into a conversation about their dogs and decided to meet the next night at the neighborhood dog run. The two dogs got along so well that they decided to become friends. At first, the conversations were always about dogs and how to care for them, what great companions they made, and where the dogs should be taken for fun. Eventually that conversation was exhausted, and it turned to other topics. When discussing every other topic, her new friend seemed to have a negative comment. She didn't really like her job, the weather was miserable, and the city they lived in had too much crime. The government was overtaxing her, her mechanic was trying to cheat her, and her cell phone service was deplorable. Suddenly, Joyce realized she was in the presence of a negative person.

As with the others, Joyce's joy was departing, and a dark mood had arrived. Immediately and without explanation, Joyce stopped seeing the woman. She did not know how to "break up" with her and so simply avoided her whenever possible. If they had a shift together, she acted distracted and busy. If the woman called, Joyce would refuse to answer the phone. First, the woman responded by making snide remarks to customers and employees about Joyce. Though they did not know who she was talking about, Joyce knew. Next, this woman would interrupt her conversations in the break room with an opposite opinion no matter what it was. Her former friend handled the store birthday celebrations, and when it was Joyce's birthday, she had suddenly written the wrong date on her calendar. So, there was absolutely no cake or decorations to celebrate in the break room. Finally, it came to a head when they found themselves in the break room alone.

The bitter woman glared at her silently and Joyce would not look at her. Eventually, the woman remarked, "What's your problem with me anyway?" Joyce could not respond. She got up and walked out of the room. Joyce had been so depressed about the whole affair that she came to see me. She seriously did not know what to do. I explained to Joyce that she had not taken the responsibility God had given her; instead, she should have gently confronted the woman. When people do not know why others reject them, they will usually fill in the blanks from their own pasts. Perhaps, she had been terribly rejected by a parent, sibling, or husband. This would only confirm in her mind something that was not true. She would become just like them, even though she is like Christ.

First, Joyce told the Lord God how sorry she was for not following His law. She should have confronted the woman and not have treated her so poorly. Then, Joyce went to the woman to make peace with her. She apologized for ignoring her and then gently confronted her. The woman's response was complete and total disbelief. She screamed loudly, "I am not a negative person!" and stormed out. When she returned, I told her she was not responsible for the other's reaction, but she was to pray and love the obstinate. Every chance she got she should show the woman love in the ways outlined in this chapter, and let the Lord do the rest. It took some time for the relationship to be reconciled, but it finally happened. Then, the two women developed a solid work relationship.

A Personal Response

Dear Heavenly Father,

I know I have done some things wrong in my relationship with (add name). I have done all I can to reconcile with him (her), now I need Your power. Please open the heart of (add name) to my restoration efforts. While Your Holy Spirit is working, I pray that you will provide me the willingness and persistence to love (add name) even though he (she) is being obstinate. I accept my responsibility for upsetting (add name) and ask that You will provide me with the patience I need. Help me to honor and glorify You in my relationship with (add name). I pray this in the name of Jesus. Amen.

Chapter 3

Battle and Rely

I am sure, it has become quite obvious that this process of conflict resolution is a challenge on many levels. There may be times where we may take several steps forward and then fall backward. The reason for this is that these steps are divine acts. Our Father is asking us in the name of His Son and through the power of the Holy Spirit to engage in pure supernatural thoughts, words, and actions. These cannot be accomplished in our humanity. This process of reconciliation will require time, a battle, and supernatural strength.

A Typical Scenario

Have you ever had or heard a conversation with a spouse, parent, or friend about their sister that went something like this? "Wow! I just finished talking to my mother and found out my sister has been bad-mouthing me to everyone in the family. Do you remember last year when I ran into that fence with my sister's car? Then we got into a disagreement about how much it should cost to repair and didn't speak to each other for two weeks. After we worked things out, I told her that I didn't want it blabbed to everyone in the family. Now, for no apparent reason, she decided to start talking about it. She blames the whole incident on me. I have had it with her. I'm finished. It's over. She is dead to me!"

Though this is an imaginary scenario, it illustrates the fact that there might be times where we really have a struggle within ourselves to resolve our disputes and make peace with others. Often, Christians have the belief that if believers were truly spiritual, they would be able to fully resolve conflicts with anybody, about anything, and at any time. Some think that this conflict resolution process should come immediately and completely for the mature saint. When it doesn't happen, these people are immature, carnal, and fleshly. This concept could not be further from the truth. The conflict resolution process may take some time to complete at any spiritual maturity level.

A Scriptural Principle

In this chapter, we discuss a biblical truth that will help us avoid putting so much pressure on ourselves or the others involved as we proceed through the reconciliation process. We now embark on the study of a principle which is often misunderstood. The third principle is "we must know that reconciliation will require supernatural strength, time, and a battle." We have seen that to restore a relationship requires a divine act on God's part in our lives. This is something that God does. It comes from His character, His power, and His Spirit. In Psalm 86:5, David cried, "For you, Lord, are good, and ready to forgive; abundant in loving kindness to all those who call on you." The Lord God's forgiveness and desire to reconcile which pours out of His loving kindness is a supernatural characteristic of deity. This truth means that we may need to be patient with ourselves and others as we all struggle with behaving in a divine way.

A Biblical Explanation

How do we build up this divinely powerful, supernatural strength to win this battle? Though not as often utilized by believers as they should be, it is primarily through God's two strength builders: the Bible and prayer. Paul explains the power of God's Word in his letter to the Thessalonian church. Paul had only been in Thessalonica for a very short time, but the gospel (God's Word) had a mighty, explosive, supernatural, and powerful effect on these believers. In 1 Thessalonians 1:5, the apostle declares, "And that our Good News came to you not in word only, but also in power, and in the Holy Spirit." The gospel came in word (this is what we read), and in power (as we live it), and in the Holy Spirit (as He enables us). The Greek word translated "power," is the Greek root word from which we get our English word "dynamite." It speaks of explosive and mighty power. And this power is the supernatural power of deity. When we read the Word and gain knowledge of God and how he desires us to act, we gain the power to live it out through His Spirit.

How does this divine power work in making peace? To build the spiritual strength needed to reconcile, we begin by reading the Bible. God's Word speaks of Him as a gracious, always merciful, compassionate, and forgiving Father who reconciles with us and desires that we reconcile with others. The Father wishes His children to act just like Him (1 Peter 1:15-16). It provides example after example of reconciliation and restoration of relationships when people sinned against believers or believers sinned against others. As we read this, we then gain the strength to live it out. It does not even necessarily have to be these truths. Any part of the Bible can be read and studied which will provide strength, since all Scripture is profitable. Usually, I read the Word until I am ready for battle! As we read, the Spirit unleashes power.

Before, during, and after this study of God's Holy Word, we should pray for strength and a willing heart to obey. We should ask God for this same strength and heart for the others involved. Paul exhorted the church at Thessalonica to "pray without ceasing" (1 Thessalonians 5:17). He simply meant that they should keep bathing their lives in prayer.

Then Paul asks, "Brothers, pray for us" (1 Thessalonians 5:25). He encouraged the Romans always to be "rejoicing in hope; enduring in troubles; continuing steadfastly in prayer" (Romans 12:12). In the midst of these difficulties, Peter declared, "But the end of all things is near. Therefore, be of sound mind, self-controlled, and sober in prayer" (1 Peter 4:7). This battle we will engage in will need a sound mind, self-control, and sober, alert prayer. We will discuss prayer as an offensive weapon later in this chapter. Suffice it to say, the Word and prayer are found together in the Scriptures. They are two sides of the same coin of power unleashed. (Acts 2:42; 6:4; 1 Timothy 4:5; 2 Thessalonians 3:1).

Once our supernatural strength is gained, we must put on the full armor of God to battle three formidable enemies which we have discussed throughout this book: the flesh, the world system, and the Devil and his demons. This armor is discussed at length by Paul in Ephesians 6:10-20. Paul begins with the supernatural strength needed to put on the armor. In Ephesians 6:10, he asserts, "Finally, be strong in the Lord and in the strength of His might." It takes strength to put on the armor and use it to battle our enemies so we may show reconcile with others.

In Ephesians 6:11, Paul commands, "Put on the full armor of God, so that you will be able to stand firm against the schemes of the devil." The Greek word translated "put on" means "sink into or put on as clothing." By faith we are to spiritually put on each and every piece of armor one at a time, just as warriors would physically put on their armor for battle. Only our armor is spiritual and divinely powerful (2 Corinthians 10:4). Why? The armor will enable us to "stand firm." Then in verse 13, he says that it will enable us to "resist" the temptation to sin. Though Paul defines here the enemy as the Devil, we also know that the Devil created an evil world system (society) run by demons that follows him. Also, within us is an enemy which is the flesh. In our context, we must stand firm against and resist temptations to sin when a conflict arises.

We must repel hardened hearts, vengeance, bitterness, anger, despair, slander and many other evils that will come about if we do not ask for or are unwilling to reconcile. In Ephesians 6:14-20, Paul reiterates his proclamations to stand firm and then describes the armor we are to put on in order to resist these temptations that the Devil throws at us. In fact, in Ephesians 6:16, Paul actually describes them as "flaming arrows of the evil one." The picture is of archers shooting arrows into a crowd of warriors to maim or kill them. Their great hope was for them to become confused, disunified, and retreat from the battle. At times, the arrows are coming so quickly that we can hardly catch our breath. We stumble and stagger spiritually and eventually fall into sin. In our context, we fall into destroying the relationship.

Each piece of armor is critical to the battle we must face. Let us look at the defensive armor first from top to bottom. Paul mentions the "helmet of salvation." The soldier had to put his helmet on to protect his head. A blow to the head by a sword would kill him instantly. This refers to the person being saved and acknowledging he or she must act as if they are saved. In Romans 13:12, Paul explains, "The night is far gone, and the day is near. Let's therefore throw off the deeds of darkness, and let's put on the armor of light." To apply this to our context, we must be saved to reconcile. We must be true Christians and understand that Christians restore relationships. Those who do not know the Lord, become angry and bitter, but that is not the way of the believer.

Second, the breastplate of righteousness should be taken up. This is generally the confession of sin and the pursuit after righteous deeds. In 2 Timothy 2:22, Paul tells Timothy,

39

"Flee from youthful lusts; but pursue righteousness, faith, love, and peace with those who call on the Lord out of a pure heart." In our context, they must pursue what is right in the Lord's reconciliation process. A "right" response would be the confession of our sins to God and to the other person. Then, they ought to pursue the "right" course of action to rebuild what was destroyed. It may also entail covering over in love or proceeding to the decision-making process. Also, we should be engaged in general righteous living. It will be much easier to reconcile than if we are involved in sinful living. Then, arguing and quarreling with others will seem out of place in our holiness. Being filled with the fruits of the Spirit will encourage us to reconcile and demonstrate grace, mercy, and compassion.

Third, soldier saints are to "gird their loins with truth" in their battle. The Roman soldier had to roll his long garb up and tighten it with a belt in order to fight. This does not refer to honesty but the knowledge and understanding of God's truth in the Scriptures. The warrior must know the truth of God and not be fooled by Satan's lies (John 8:44). In 1 John 2:14, the apostle describes those who are spiritually mature, "I have written to you, fathers, because you know him who is from the beginning. I have written to you, young men, because you are strong, and the word of God remains in you, and you have overcome the evil one." These spiritually mature saints knew the Word and were able to "overcome the Evil One." The Greek word translated "overcome" means "to conquer or prevail against someone or something." We must know the Word because the flesh, and the World, and the Devil will lie to us. They will encourage us to become angry and bitter and "stand up for our rights" and "pay them back for what they did." In our context, they must know the truth well enough to be able to discern at every point what the Truth says about the issue and what is the proper godly response. We discern the lies and know how to handle them.

Fourth, God's warrior must have the appropriate shoes. His feet must be "shod with the gospel of peace." The Roman soldier wore a cleat-like shoe into battle, so he could never lose his footing. These special shoes had spikes under them to entrench the feet into the ground for balance in the time of battle. These are similar to the cleats a football player wears on the football field. They utilize them for much needed traction and balance. This refers to the full understanding of the gospel and the regular and consistent sharing of it. When one is interested in winning people to Christ, they are much more sensitive to their words and actions in their different relationships. They are more cognizant of the importance of being an example of what a person looks like and how they act when Christ is in their lives. They will go out of their way not to offend them as they are attempting to share the gospel with the person, they may have the issue with.

In 1 Corinthians 10:32-33, the apostle encourages, "Give no occasions for stumbling, either to Jews, or to Greeks, or to the assembly of God." He did not want to make any of the people he was in contact with stumble in anyway. Why? He adds, "Even as I also please all men in all things, not seeking my own profit, but the profit of the many, that they may be saved." He wanted to see them saved. In our context, we may be attempting to share Christ with the person we have a relationship with. We do not want to offend them with anger or bitterness or some transgression against them so we can present to them the good news of peace. Perhaps, the people with whom we are sharing Christ are watching how we relate to our spouses, children, friends, or co-workers. If they always see us fighting and arguing with others, they might not listen to the gospel. Why would they want to come to Christ, when it does not change their lives?

Fifth, these spiritual warriors are to defend themselves with "the shield of faith." These shields were big enough to hide behind and to take the blows of a sword. They were covered with pitch and could immediately extinguish all the flaming arrows of an enemy archer. This refers to Christians who live their lives based on faith, not experience or feeling. They believe in the Bible and live by its principles. They do not depend on how they feel when they are in battle or what they are experiencing. In 1 Peter 5:9, Peter explains that our enemy, the Devil, is a roaring lion prowling about hungry to devour the saints. He exhorts us to "withstand him steadfast in your faith, knowing that your brothers who are in the world are undergoing the same sufferings."

We must battle with a grounded, steadfast faith believing in God's Word and His power to fulfill all of its principles. In our context, we disregard our feelings or experiences and follow God's laws in reconciliation. We believe that if we follow God's blueprint, we will be successful in restoring the relationship or obeying the will of God if He has different plans. If the Lord says to make peace, then we believe Him and make peace. We do not wait for our feelings to catch up and match our obedience. If we are afraid the person may not respond, we should begin the process anyway. We ought to repent and let God work in the other person's life. Even when we do not emotionally "feel" like it, we will build bridges to restore the relationship by faith.

There are also two offensive weapons for our numerous spiritual battles. The first is "the sword of the spirit, which is the Word of God." The Greek word translated "Word" means specific utterances of the Word. In 1 Peter 1:25, Peter uses the same word when he writes, "'But the Word of the Lord endures forever.' And this is the word which was preached to you." This refers to the specific preached words of the Scriptures. A warrior in battle is always attacking with his sword. In Matthew 4, each temptation of the Devil was met with a very specific verse from the Scriptures. We battle the rationalizations of the flesh with the truth of Scriptures. We should have a conversation within ourselves between the old man (the flesh in our bodies) and the new man (our true selves in Christ). We should compare our thoughts, words, and actions with biblical principles.

In our context, we stand against our flesh and say in our minds that we are saved (helmet of salvation) and now live for God. He desires for us to reconcile and make peace with others. This is what God desires, and we will obey. The flesh will counter with all kinds of reasons why we shouldn't act like God. We must then decide who we will follow: God or our flesh, our new master or old master. While we do this, we pray for resistance. In 1 Corinthians 9:26-27, this is what Paul meant when he said, "I fight like that, as not beating the air, but I beat my body and bring it into submission, lest by any means, after I have preached to others, I myself should be rejected." Paul fought with his own body (his flesh) to get it under control so he would never do something sinful to disqualify himself from ministry.

The second offensive weapon is prayer. I like to call it the spear of prayer, though Paul simply adds it in at the end. In Ephesians 6:18-20, he implored, "With all prayer and petition pray at all times in the Spirit, and with this in view, be on the alert with all perseverance and petition for all the saints, and pray on my behalf, that utterance may be given to me in the opening of my mouth, to make known with boldness the mystery of the gospel." In the midst of the battle the warrior is communicating constantly with the commander and with the other warriors in battle. Each is supporting the other as they follow the commands of their leader. When we need help, we ask for it, when others need help, they ask us. In 1 Thessalonians 5:25, in the midst of the raging battle with the forces of evil, Paul cried out, "Brothers, pray for us." In Romans 1:9, he adds, "For God is my witness, whom I serve in my spirit in the Good News of his Son, how unceasingly I make mention of you always in my prayers." As the apostle Paul was battling and they were battling, both of them were praying for each other.

In our context, as warriors, we pray for victory against the flesh and assistance in the reconciliation process. If we are the transgressors, we should pray that God would give us the needed strength to resist our flesh and seek peace with the ones we have transgressed. With the smaller issues we beg for patience and with larger we cry out for courage to go to the decision-making process. If we are transgressed, we request that God would soften the hearts of the others and move them to repentance through His Spirit. We should also pray that God would help us forgive them and at least seek peace from our side whether they repent or not. Our prayers should also entail the control of our anger which can easily arise. Then, we continue our battle and rely on the Spirit.

An Ancient Portrait

An example of this battle against sin, though ultimately lost, is the story of Cain and Abel in Genesis four. Here we see the battle up close. Once Adam and Eve sinned, they were basically thrown out of the garden. Cain was the first one born out of the union between these two people. After his brother Abel was born, we are not told much about the two brothers, except that Abel kept flocks and his brother Cain farmed. By this time, Adam had taught his children that God desired a blood sacrifice in order to properly worship Him. When it came time to bring an offering to the Lord, Cain brought the first fruits of his crops. That made perfect sense because Cain was a farmer. Abel brought the first of his flocks and their fat portions. That made sense because Abel was a shepherd and cattleman.

Yet, the Lord had no regard for Cain's offering. Why? In Hebrews 11:4, the author illuminates the situation, "By faith, Abel offered to God a more excellent sacrifice than Cain, through which he had testimony given to him that he was righteous, God testifying with respect to his gifts; and through it he, being dead, still speaks." When God accepted the gifts of Abel, He was confirming the true faith that Abel had toward Him. Abel's true faith produced a righteous life which brought the recognition of his sin and the need for repentance.

The true believer then acts in accordance with how God desires him to present himself before the Lord. In this case, it was through a blood sacrifice. Cain, on the other hand, was an unrighteous man coming to the Lord in his own "good" works. In 1 John 3:12, John gets to the heart of Cain's problem, when he says, "Unlike Cain, who was of the evil one, and killed his brother." Cain was of the Devil. He did not follow God in faith. Instead, he followed the Devil and did as the Devil did. Then the apostle adds, "Why did he kill him? Because his deeds were evil, and his brother's righteous." Cain did bring the best of what he grew, but it was not what God desired. It was what Cain desired.

We cannot get to God in our own way! Cain attempted to get to God through his own good deeds. When the offerings came, God was pleased with Abel's faith-based offering but would not accept Cain's prideful rebellious offering. So, Cain immediately became angry because his younger brother was righteous, and he was evil. Wickedness hates righteousness, so Cain became sullen, and it could be clearly seen. Then, the Lord spoke to Cain and asked him why he was so angry and why had his face become so sullen. God provided a chance for Cain to repent of his anger and the improper sacrifice. So, he could offer the proper one. He needed only to repent, believe, and show his belief through a blood sacrifice.

God told Cain to go and do well; then, he would not feel anger but joy. The solution was so simple. Don't be angry at your brother because I wouldn't accept the sacrifice, simply go and get the proper sacrifice. Then He issues a warning. He tells him sin is crouching at the door and desires to take him over. Sin like a hungry animal is crouching and waiting for the opportune time to pounce on him and take control of him. He urged Cain to master it. He must get control of his flesh, his anger, and his rebellion. Here is the battle with the flesh. He provides a choice that we all have. Do we want to do well or not? The real issue is who is going to be our master? Sin or God? Will it be our desires or God's desires? Unfortunately, sin's desires overcame evil Cain but should not with us.

Then Cain lured his brother into a field where no one was around. While they were alone, Cain killed his brother. After this, the Lord asked Cain where his brother was. Of course, the Lord God knew, but He was providing an opportunity for Cain to repent once again. Cain should have said, "He's gone Lord, and I killed him. God, I am so sorry." Instead, he sarcastically responded, "I do not know. Am I my brother's keeper?" Then the Lord cried, "What have you done?" This was an opportunity to repent. Then God told him that Abel's blood was crying out to Him. God knew exactly what he had done, and Abel's blood was the real witness of his murder. In His justice, God curses the ground which Cain depended upon for his sustenance. Cain took Adam's son away, now God was going to take Cain's livelihood away. The ground will be cursed because it bears the body of Abel. The ground would no longer grow crops for him, he would have to wander upon the earth, and then become a vagrant.

He knew that once people found out about his curse, they would kill him. In God's mercy, He placed a mark on his forehead and proclaimed that whoever killed Cain, His vengeance would be on him sevenfold. Why? God decides the sentence alone, not an individual. This would be both a mark of disdain and protection. Notice, he did not ask for forgiveness nor seek peace. So, Moses writes that Cain went out from the presence of the Lord and settled in the land of Nod. What a great example of the battle with the flesh even though Cain lost that battle.

Cain did have the Lord God's presence to encourage him to stand against the flesh, but we have God's Spirit inside of us. Which is better? God spoke to him directly, but God also speaks to us directly through His Word. In our context of reconciliation, we need to repent of our sinful actions which lead to relationship issues. Then, we pray and read the Word to acquire the power that we need to restore the relationship using the armor of God. We must put on the armor so we will win the battle against the flesh, the world, and the Devil. They do not want relationships to be whole but broken or destroyed. Christians need to reconcile their relationships through God's strength. This is God's blueprint.

A Modern Anecdote

Christians are required to reconcile all their relationships, including those of co-workers. This is often neglected, yet problems with people we work with abound. Everyone has a story about a problem with their boss or fellow worker. One such man walked into my office slumped over in defeat and brokenness. He was a new teacher at his school, and He had tried with great effort and difficulty to solve a problem that he had with the fifth-grade teacher next door. It all started with a red ball. The rule in the elementary school was that only yellow balls could be used for kick ball because they were thicker and could endure the physical abuse. Because they were thinner, the red balls were to be used for playing catch, foursquare, and handball. When he came to the school the classroom had no yellow balls. He was very concerned about his students being able to play kickball. This had been his favorite game in grade school. He wanted to use it for P.E. and teach the children some cool tricks he had learned.

When he had ordered the yellow balls from the district, he discovered that they were on back order. He couldn't find one yellow ball to use in the school. Only four classrooms had them, and they didn't want them kicked over the fence, lost, or popped. So they would not loan them out to this new teacher. The man ordered several red balls. Since there were no yellow balls, his class would use the red ball to kick. He did not think much of it because he used his class money. It seemed like such a mundane thing to him, and he felt that rules were to serve people, not for people to serve the rules. Nobody said anything as he played kickball at his P.E. period. Then one day, the students begged him to allow them to use the red ball at recess because there were no yellow balls to kick during that time. Thinking this should not be a problem, he allowed it.

When recess was over, the teacher next door stomped up to him while both classes were lined up next to each other and yelled, "Mr. Jackson [not his real name], your class was kicking a red ball. That is against the rules." With complete surprise, he calmly responded by explaining the problem and his solution." She starred at him and shouted, "Rules are rules. They must be followed by everyone." This made him angry, so he shouted his response that rules are meant to serve people and not the other way around. She glared at him and then shouted at her class to follow her; then, they went off to her classroom. It wasn't long before this man was somewhat of a celebrity in the school because he was kind, funny, an enthusiastic teacher, and interested in school being a place the children wanted to be.

This only added fuel to the hot fire. A few weeks later, he discovered that she was constantly complaining about him to their principal, back-biting him in the lunchroom, and criticizing him to her class. This had to stop. He stormed into her empty classroom one day after school and blasted, "Why don't you get a life and just leave me alone." An argument ensued, and he marched out. This continued for over three months. She would complain, back-bite, and criticize him; then, he would storm in and blast her. Until one day, he was reading the Scriptures at home and read several passages on reconciling as God has reconciled with us. The Holy Spirit convicted him at that moment so powerfully that he felt a huge weight was now leaning on his shoulders. He did not know exactly what to do. He had found himself in a vicious cycle and did not know how to get out of it.

I explained to him that he had to reconcile with her. He had to go and apologize for his part in the situation and resolve the conflict. Then he had to build a relationship that would honor the Lord. He told me that he didn't think he could do it. I explained that it would take spiritual strength, time, and a battle with his flesh. I described the armor of God and explained how to put it on with her. It took him three weeks of prayer and study of the Word to approach her.

The first encounter turned once again into an argument. The second encounter he opened the door of her classroom, shook his head, and walked out. The third time, he had a pleasant conversation but couldn't get himself to apologize. Finally, the man had enough spiritual strength to walk into her classroom and apologize. She sat silent. Over several months, he followed God's blueprint of reconciliation. The result was the building of a God-honoring work relationship with her. He was not required to have anything deeper if he did not desire it. This would be enough.

A Personal Response

Dear Heavenly Father,

I suddenly recognized the battle that I am in concerning my relationship with (add name). I have not been winning it. Instead, I have done many things to disrupt Your plan of reconciliation (list the things). I am truly sorry. Help me to go to Your Word and prayer to find the strength in Your Spirit I need to put on Your full armor of light. My flesh is obstinate, the world encourages strife, and the Devil relishes in it. Yet, Your Word tells me that You desire reconciliation leading to relationships that honor and glorify You. Fill me with the courage to take the first step to restore what has been broken with (add name). Please move (add name) to respond to my loving gestures. I pray this in the name of Jesus. Amen.

Chapter 4

Act Like Him

If you finished these two conflict resolution books, then you possess all the tools needed to make a relationship last a lifetime. Wait a minute, isn't that what we hope relationships will do? Don't we wish for them to last a lifetime? Isn't that what the Lord desires for marriage relationships to do? Does not our Father command that they have lifelong covenants? Why aren't they? To possess the tools is not enough, both people must utilize them. For this to happen, only one more issue needs discussion. Will you do it? Many people leave my office with exactly the same bag of tools to repair their relationships and yet some crash and burn and others go on to live very happy fulfilled lives in their marriages, families, friendships, churches, and other various partnerships. What makes the difference? It is the motivation and desire to obey God. What makes one person utilize the tools I have given them from God's Word and the other not? It is the genuine willingness to follow the Lord, the serious commitment to submit to all His commands, and the absolute desire to live like Him and His Son through His Holy Spirit.

A Typical Scenario

Have you ever had or heard a conversation with a spouse to a friend that went something like this? "No, it is over. I am done with this marriage. Yes, I went to counseling with him and I know what to do, but I don't want to do it. Too many things have happened. (Friend responds.) I do not care what the Bible says. I am extremely unhappy, and that's all there is to it (Friend responds.) Yes, I have seen some change, but it is too little, too late. I went to another counselor, and she told me that I should look out for my own emotional well-being, so I am. (Friend responds.) The children will be fine. Divorce is very common today. They will still get to see their father every other weekend and holidays. (Friend responds.) Yes, they cried and cried, but I told them that they would be much happier if mommy and daddy weren't fighting all the time. (Friend responds.) What about my church's reaction? If they give me any trouble, I will just find another one. When I walk into the next one, I will just tell them I'm divorced."

This scenario is typical of many people as they rationalize their destruction of their lifelong covenant. Many of these people do have deep wounds from their relationships, but they can be restored using the tools from Scripture. If both are Christians, their main desire for restoration should be to live like their Lord. If God had abandoned us, we would be on our way to hell. Yet, God has made a lifelong covenant with us; He constantly forgives and seeks reconciliation with us regardless of what we do. Then, God desires us to do the same to others.

A Scriptural Principle

This chapter discusses the next principle in this critical reconciliation process. This principle involves the motivation for doing it. Let's face it, this can be an extremely difficult process because not only do we make numerous mistakes, but so does our partner. We must have some serious reasons for engaging in the restoration process because it is so easy to give up and start over. This brings us to principle four which is "we must resolve conflicts because we must act just like God." This may seem simple or even a bit strange as a motivation because it is not geared toward our betterment or the fulfillment of our needs. It involves the honoring and glorifying of God. Our motivation is all about God and only secondarily about us. It is the opposite of the world's desire to revolve itself around the individual and their needs. We want everything to be about us - our needs, our wants, our lives. This is not how God works. The motivation of "acting like Him" is deeply spiritual, powerfully supernatural and is what the Holy Spirit thrives on in a believer's life. When our lives revolve around God and what He desires, supernatural things happen.

A Biblical Explanation

To comprehend why we as Christians must reconcile our broken relationships, we must understand the very person of the God who sent His only Son to die in order to forgive and reconcile the broken relationship we had with Him. We must understand His character that brought forth the love, grace, and mercy demonstrated in the work that had to be accomplished to restore our relationship that we had with Him in the garden. This knowledge will bring the desire to utilize these tools that have been presented in this book from the Scriptures and will become the driving force in our own resolution of relational conflicts. We will approach God in our discussion from His Triune essence as Father, Son, and Holy Spirit.

The attributes and qualities possessed by the persons of the Godhead which drove them to redeem us in spite of our rebellion provide not only the example of what we are to do but the motivation for doing it. When God adopts us into His family, He expects us to behave like Him, follow His blueprint by obeying His commands, and accept fully His holy reign in our lives. Good fathers desire their children to follow in their footsteps, want them to obey, and accept their authority. These are some of the many reasons which drive and motivate Christians to reconcile with others; we must discuss each carefully providing the Spirit with the truth He needs to unleash His power in our lives to make peace with others. The supernatural work that the Lord asks us as His children to accomplish in our relationships with one another and those outside the faith involve the gracious attitudes and actions which He Himself showed us. We must feel compelled to demonstrate the same to others. The old adage becomes all too true with the Godhead: "Like Father, like Son (Jesus)." Then, perhaps we might continue, "Like Father, like sons (us)." As God's supernatural offspring, we act like Him.

First, we must behave like God. In the time of the prophet Micah, the Hebrew people had fallen into sin. Like the two prophets who prophesied at around the same time, Isaiah and Hosea, Micah preached a true message of God's divine judgment and deliverance. Not only did our God discipline His people for their constant idolatry and iniquity, but He brought reconciliation and great blessing once they finally turned back to Him. In Micah 7:18-19, Micah proclaimed, "Who is a God like you, who pardons iniquity, and passes over the disobedience of the remnant of his heritage?" The prophet is reveling in the difference between His God and the false gods round about him. Then he marvels, "He [God] doesn't retain his anger forever, because he [God] delights in loving kindness. He [God] will again have compassion on us. He [God] will tread our iniquities under foot; and you [God] will cast all their [our] sins into the depths of the sea. You [God] will give truth to Jacob, and mercy to Abraham, [and their offspring - us] as you have sworn to our fathers from the days of old."

After explaining to the Hebrews the coming judgment of God, he also describes the Lord's subsequent willingness to reconcile. Then the prophet pauses to marvel at the amazing character of the one, true Deity in the universe. He asks, "Who is a God like you, who pardons iniquity?" The answer of course is no one. No god is like our God. You cannot even make up a god like Him. In Daniel 9:9, the prophet declares, "To the Lord our God belong mercies and forgiveness." The source of all reconciliation with others proceeds from the divine holy, loving, gracious, and merciful character of God, and there is no one like Him. Many times, in the Scriptures, we are commanded to think and act like our Father.

Here is a critical point: the seeking of peace that believers must show toward others will demonstrate God's holy character as He works in them. In 1 Peter 1:15-16, the apostle Peter exclaims this, "But just as he who called you is holy, you yourselves also be holy in all of your behavior." Just as our Father is holy in His behavior, His children are to be in theirs. Then the apostle quotes an extremely familiar Old Testament passage to the Jews, "Because it is written, "You shall be holy; for I am holy." This important Greek word translated "holy" means "set apart." We might think of it as "separate from or wholly different from" men.

Therefore, our Lord expects His children to be "set apart, separate, or wholly different" from the world around them in their thinking, feeling, and behaving. This is not easy. It requires much time in the Word, prayer, and spending time among believers who think, feel, and act this same way. One of the holy ways of God is reconciliation. Though the world may harbor deep bitterness, we reconcile. Though the world might demand a set of actions to restore relationships, we do not. Since the Lord makes peace with us, we act in the same manner and make peace with others. Since the Lord seeks peace with all men, so do we. We, as saints, are to behave wholly differently, and this demonstrates that we are the true children of God. This is such an important divine truth that should motivate Christians to reconcile.

Our Lord Jesus appeals to this principle in His discussion of the love of enemies. He explains that anyone can love someone who loves him, but people in God's kingdom love those who do not love them. Our God provides the sunshine and rain to demonstrate His great love toward all people. In Matthew 5:48, He proclaims, "Therefore you shall be perfect, just as your Father in heaven is perfect." We can also apply this general principle to others in the restoration process. Just as the Lord reconciles with others, so we are to do the exact same thing. In Matthew 6:12, the Lord teaches that prayer should include these words, "Forgive us our debts, as we also forgive our debtors." The confession of our sins to our Father should include the loving attitude of forgiveness (reconciliation is the natural result) that we are asking Him for towards others.

In Ephesians 4:31-32, concerning believers Paul declares, "Let all bitterness, wrath, anger, outcry, and slander, be put away from you, with all malice." We must continually be putting away these conflict producing attitudes. Then Paul continues with these words, "And be kind to one another, tenderhearted, forgiving each other, just as God also in Christ forgave you." We should then be continually putting on these conflict resolving attitudes. As God is pouring out His forgiveness and making peace upon us every day of our lives, we should be pouring out our forgiveness and making peace with others every day of their lives.

This will result in reconciliation and restoration. Why is this critical? When we reconcile, we act like our Father, God. When we remember that the Lord is constantly restoring our relationships to Him, this should motivate us to take the steps necessary for reconciliation. It takes the character of God and the desire to behave like Him to seek peace if we have been transgressed or we have been the transgressor because it is at times so difficult to desire to make peace.

56

Second, this will require a commitment to following the Lord God's blueprint. The Lord God has only one plan for the healing of relationships that are broken. It is to reconcile. In Matthew 5:23-24, Jesus describes the process believers must use if they have transgressed someone. He exhorts, "If therefore you are offering your gift at the altar, and there remember that your brother has anything against you, leave your gift there before the altar, and go your way. First be reconciled to your brother...then come and offer your gift."

Later, in Matthew 18:15, the Lord Jesus describes the process believers must use if they have been transgressed by someone. He explains, "If your brother sins against you, go, show him his fault between you and him alone. If he listens to you, you have gained back your brother." In both these passages, we are told to reconcile relationships with those people who might have something against us, or we have something against them. Christians ought to reconcile with them. When true believers have a broken relationship with parents, spouses, children, friends, neighbors, acquaintances, fellow students, church members, and co-workers, they should go to them directly and reconcile the relationship.

Since God is the creator of the universe and originator of man and all of His fundamental relationships, He knows the best way to preserve or heal those relationships. We must realize that His way is often times very different than man's way. In Isaiah 55:8-11, the Lord God declares about Himself, "'For my thoughts are not your thoughts, and your ways are not my ways,' says Yahweh. 'For as the heavens are higher than the earth, so are my ways higher than your ways, and my thoughts than your thoughts.'" He is very different from mankind. This is why forgiveness and reconciliation seem so foreign to us. It is only foreign to our flesh, not our Spirit. The Lord God continues, "For as the rain comes down and the snow from the sky, and doesn't return there, but waters the earth, and makes it grow and bud, and gives seed to the sower and bread to the eater."

The Lord God Almighty compares His Word and to the rain. An analogy everyone can understand. The rain always accomplishes what He designed it to do. It produces growth in the land and provides sustenance for mankind. Just as sure as the effect of rain is on earth, so is God's Word. The Lord God states, "So is my word that goes out of my mouth: it will not return to me void, but it will accomplish that which I please, and it will prosper in the thing I sent it to do." In His Word, He provides commands that deal with every area of relationships. One of these is when they go awry. If we follow the Lord's blueprint, which may be very different than what we would desire to do, the Word will do its work. It will not come up void. We can trust that the relationship will be reestablished. Yet, God may at times allow the destruction of a relationship. As long as we follow God's blueprint, we can be assured that His will is done. We can only do our part which is to attempt a reconciliation.

Third, we must also accept His reign in our lives. One of the key barriers to restoring relationships with others is feeling victimized by people. We do not want to reconcile because we feel that we are victims of others. This creates in us an anger that is difficult to remove. This stands in the way of any kind of restoration attempt. Yet, we should recognize God's sovereignty in allowing the sinful actions we are to deal with. When people sin against us, they must be allowed to do that by God. Job said it best when he told his wife in Job 2:10, "But he said to her, 'You speak as one of the foolish women speaks. Shall we indeed accept good from God and not adversity?' In all this, Job did not sin with his lips." Notice, that comment by Job was true. He did not sin by telling a falsehood with His lips. Yet, it was Satan that hurt, maimed, and "victimized" him. Righteous Job did not view the situation this way. He recognized the reign of God over the whole earth and accepted it. Satan had to ask permission.

When people sin against us, it must be allowed by God. They cannot victimize us. They can become instruments of God's work in our lives as the Lord brings trials among us, but nobody sneaks by Him to hurt or harm us. This is such a critical point. Since God is in charge, we are not anyone's victim. This was so clearly indicated by Jesus at his arrest. Peter decided to intervene and drew his sword to fight the crowd and cut the ear off one of the servants. Jesus told him to put his sword down. Then in Matthew 26:53, He asks Peter, "Do you think that I cannot appeal to My Father, and He will at once put at My disposal more than twelve legions of angels?" God was in control. He always had been from the moment Jesus was born, and He was no victim. The Father had allowed them to act. He could intervene at any time. When someone sins against us, God has allowed it. We see this when Jesus stood before the great Pontius Pilate. In John 19:10, John records, "Pilate therefore said to Him, 'You do not speak to me? Do you not know I have authority to release You and I have authority to crucify you?'"

Pilate thought he was in control of the Lord. He thought he had the authority to decide whether Jesus would live or die. In John 11:11, Jesus sets him straight, "Jesus answered him, 'You would have no authority over Me, unless it had been given you from above.'" He was a powerful man, but he couldn't do anything without the approval of God. Can we as Christians please let God be sovereign over us? The Lord claims that He is in total and complete control of all things including the consequences of sin. He claims He can directly cause something, or He can also allow something to occur. He claims that He is in charge. Will we please trust in what He says? We are not victims, but we are servants of a living God. Throw off the victim mentality and seek peace.

An Ancient Portrait

Two great examples of this principle are Jesus Christ as He patterned His forgiveness after the Father and Stephen as He followed his Lord Jesus the same way. This forgiveness brought the ultimate reconciliation. In Luke 23:34, the Lord was hanging on the cross, dripping with blood from the crown of thorns and the nails in his hands and feet. In His excruciating pain from the tortures and violent beatings, agonizing in the slow dying process, humiliated from the mocking of the people, He cried to His Father God to forgive these ignorant persecutors. Who were they?

The Romans, who were doing all the dirty work the Jews could not do, did not realize that they were really crucifying the ultimate King of Kings and Lord of Lords. The common Jews, who were standing around the cross throwing insults at the Lord, could not fully understand that their longed-for Messiah, was hanging from that cursed tree. The frightened disciples who had scattered from the mob could not fully comprehend that their great moment of victory in salvation had not been lost in that dying man. Instead, it was about to be completed when the price was paid, and Christ had risen from the dead. Even, many of the rulers, who were caught up in their self-righteous pride, could not perceive that the veil of the temple was about to be split into two. The lamb would be sacrificed, and the new eternal high priest would enter the Holy of Holies to represent them before the Father in heaven.

In the midst of his deep pain, Christ knowing all of this, looked down with great compassion, and cried out for the Father's forgiveness. Christians know through their study of the Scriptures that the prayer could only be fulfilled if all of these ignorant, hardhearted persecutors and enemies of the cross received the soon to be risen Son of God as Savior and

Lord. Yet, implied in the merciful cry to His Father, is a God who became truly man, and as man forgave His persecutors, tormentors, and scoffers.

Then, near the moment of His own death, He forgave the repentant thief hanging next to him as he turned to the Lord for salvation. In Luke 23:35-43, the Lord Jesus was hanging on the cross while two others were being crucified next to him. These were real criminals on either side of Him, not a God-Man. They too were hurling the same kind of abuse as those below. Like the people all around Jesus, these two thieves were hurling insults at Jesus for claiming to be the Christ, the chosen one of God, the long-awaited Messiah, and the one who fulfilled all the prophecies from ancient days. Yet, he could not save Himself from such a despicable fate.

Suddenly, one of the two thieves grew silent as the other continued his mockery. Then he prepared himself for death and considered his wicked life. He saw before his own eyes a perfect and innocent man. He must have taken a moment to ponder the very words he had spoken about Jesus' deity, the sign of His dignity, and the belief of His disciples in His divinity that was on display before them. In that moment, through the power of the Holy Spirit his blinders from Satan fell off, his prideful rationalizations for his own sins tumbled from his broken flesh, then he repented and believed. He grew sorrowful and mournful for his sins and believed that Jesus was indeed who He claimed to be. He was the Son of the living God and Savior of the world. Then deep within his heart he submitted to His Lordship.

Moments before this, the thief had cursed and criticized Jesus, now he turned toward the other thief and robber and cried out for him to cease from his abusive words. The thief declared that they deserved everything they had gotten, but

Jesus had done nothing wicked His whole life. Through this, the thief affirmed his new belief that Jesus was a righteous and holy God. Before Him, these two criminals were utterly without merit.

He questioned the other condemned outlaw as to whether he feared God. Judgment was coming; it was at their door. The physical life was draining from their bodies, and their eternal spirits would face an almighty God. As Jews, they knew the law and would have a greater judgment than the Gentiles. They had lived sin filled lives and now had been blaspheming God's anointed Messiah. The condemnation would be unimaginable. This other thief must stop before he says anything else to make his damnation even worse.

Then he turned toward Jesus Christ and asked the saving question that demonstrated all that the Holy Spirit had done in His life. He asked the Lord to remember him when He came into His Kingdom. There it was: a recognition of who Jesus was and what He was doing on the cross that day. He was not saving Himself so He could save others, and the thief desperately desired that deliverance. So, at the moment of his death, the man cried out for forgiveness and salvation. When Jesus gives up His spirit and enters the abode of His Father will He please remember this repentant criminal and bring his unworthy soul into His heaven. As the life was slowly pouring out of Him, Jesus looked at the man and declared on that very day this repentant sinner and now true saint would be with Him in paradise.

Later, in Acts 7:54-59, Stephen, a disciple, preached before the Sanhedrin and indicted them for their hypocritical sin. They responded by rushing him, dragging him out of the city, and stoning him to death. In verse 60, Luke records Stephen's Christ-like and God the Father-like response, "He kneeled down, and cried with a loud voice, 'Lord, don't hold this sin against them!' When he had said this, he fell asleep." In his final words in Acts 7:60, Stephen took up Jesus Christ's compassionate mantle and begged God for their forgiveness.

All Christians are compelled by their Lord and Savior to forgive anyone and everyone, believer or unbeliever, friend or foe, brother or acquaintance, and persecutor or supporter for any and all transgressions! This leads to reconciliation and is not human; instead, it is a supernatural phenomenon. In the gospels and epistles, it clearly states that saints are to forgive both other believers and unbelievers. Christians are to seek peace with others. Why? Saints are to act like their Father and Lord who also forgives everything at salvation eternally and continually afterward relationally. Though this is not the only step in reconciliation, it is the critical one. We must desire to forgive the sins of our enemies.

A Modern Anecdote

A medical doctor entered my office with a great sense of frustration concerning a colleague of his. They had been best friends for as long as he could remember. His parents had moved to another state when he was in middle school, and they had kept in touch for years. Both had entered medical school and had specialized in pediatrics. Both ended up in a large town near my office. Once they had both settled into their practices, they took up where they had left off.

They played rounds of golf together, attended numerous conferences and trainings, and consulted on each other's patients. Their families attended the same church and went on vacation every year together and their wives and kids had become very close. The problem began when his friend received an award from a prestigious medical association. This made him feel uneasy, but he brushed it off.

Then his physician friend was selected as one of the top ten doctors by a magazine in their city. Now he knew that his friend was an excellent pediatrician, but this was simply too much. Why wasn't he the one selected? Once his friend had an article in the magazine, his private practice suddenly took on a tidal wave of patients. This was too much for my counselee to bear. For the first time in his life, he experienced envy and jealousy.

This quickly brought forth deep within his heart a sense of resentment. His first response was to pretend that nothing was wrong. Then, he could not make their usual golf game. Since he had to attend the conference late, he suggested that they shouldn't share their usual room. At the conference, he did everything he could do to avoid this award-winning friend. The worst part was that his dear friend was receiving an enormous amount of attention. This only frustrated him even more and produced an anger that he also had never felt before. When vacation planning started, he suggested to his wife that they do something different this next year. She refused, and a fight ensued. When she demanded that he explain himself, he couldn't reveal his feelings. How could this man explain his envy, jealousy, resentment, and anger toward such a dear friend? Unfortunately, during the entire vacation he barely spoke to him. He always provided a wide variety of excuses which simply did not add up.

Then another emotion entered the scene: bitterness. Not toward his friend but toward God. Why had God allowed this to happen? Why was God playing favorites? He was as strong a Christian as his friend. Why does his friend get the recognition for which he had longed? When this bitterness took root, he stopped attending church, men's group, and reading the Bible and praying. Now his wife stepped in and begged him to see me. I took him to several passages in the Scriptures. We discussed how James and John asked to sit on either side of Jesus in His kingdom (Matthew 20:20-22). We perused the story of his disciples arguing over who would be greatest in His kingdom (Luke 9:46). We even studied the fact that careers and achievement are not the focus of God's attention but instead seeking first His kingdom (Matthew 6:33).

Finally, we studied the parable of the day laborers told by Jesus (Matthew 20:1-16). Some had worked a full day and others worked only an hour, God decided they would both get the same wages (heaven). Since the Lord decides how He blesses, when He blesses, and whom He blesses, we should be grateful for anything we are given since we truly deserve nothing. He began to realize that he was not behaving like his Father, imitating the Son, or walking in the Spirit. He was not acting "wholly separated" from those who do not know Christ. He was supposed to be holy. The Lord Jesus Christ did not seek the world's achievement but God's favor. He was to do the same. Once he realized what he had done, he had to take the next step which was to go and reconcile with his Father in heaven and his friend on earth.

A Personal Response

Dear Heavenly Father,

I acknowledge that You greatly desire for Your children to act like You. In my relationship with (add name), I answer to You, My Lord and Master. I have made some mistakes in my relationship with (add name). I am truly sorry. I need your power to take all of these biblical principles and follow them with (add name). When I sin against (add name), I know I must reconcile with him (her). Help me to behave like You and imitate Your Son in the power of the Spirit. I do want to follow Your blueprint by obeying Your commands which includes sacrificing for (add name). Please help me to accept Your reign fully in my life and relationship with him (her). May I honor you as I consistently seek to reconcile my relationship with (add name) when it begins to crumble even in the smallest way. I pray this in the name of Jesus. Amen.

Conclusion

As we conclude this book, I would like to leave us with some final thoughts about our God of reconciliation and what His Son did on the cross for us. First, if we understand the full extent of what was wrought for us on that cursed tree in order to make peace with us, it will become so much easier to do the same thing for others. Second, if you read this entire book and realized that you do not understand salvation or have never received Christ as Lord and Savior, then I would like to provide that opportunity. Please do not skip this section; it may be the most important in your life.

From all outward appearances, humans seem "good" and attempt to live decent lives. This is man's concept of himself. This is not God's concept. The Almighty's view is that people all over the world and throughout the ages sin, sin, and sin again (Romans 3:23). This is a terrible and utterly destructive condition. Yet, they have ramifications that are far worse. These sins condemn us to everlasting divine retribution.

Though described briefly in the Old Testament, the Lord Jesus Christ clearly announced and proclaimed the future punishment to come. Contrary to popular belief, Jesus did not only speak of love, grace, and mercy, He also spoke of the coming judgment for sin. He declared that the judgment of sin would be everlasting punishment in a place He called "Hell." The Lord portrayed this place as an eternal inferno (Matthew 18:8) where there would be the weeping (from the sorrow) and gnashing of teeth (from the agony and anguish of suffering) continually into eternity (Matthew 8:12; 13:42, 50; 22:13; 24:51; 25:30; Luke 13:28).

Why must people face this horrific punishment? Though God is a God of love, grace, and mercy, He is also a God of great holiness, righteousness, and justice (Psalm 89:14,18). These attributes are just as much a part of His divine nature as His love, grace, and mercy. You have broken God's law as we all have, and the penalty must be paid. This began with the first man Adam (Genesis 3:1-7). When this occurred, His love, grace, and mercy surfaced, and a provision was made. Someone else would have to take man's place and pay the penalty. Someone who had never transgressed Him, who would never deserve punishment, and would fulfill all of God's Laws, would be substituted in man's place. This was the Son of God, Jesus Christ.

As the God-Man, He would pay the penalty for our sins in His death on the cross. Once done, the Lord God made only one provision for people to appropriate what His Son had done on the cross for them. This provision is receiving Jesus Christ as Savior and Lord. Though I cannot possibly share with you this good news in the confines of this book, I would love for you to consider purchasing my book entitled, *Finding The Light: The Kingdom of Heaven and How To Enter It*. It can be found for sale on Amazon.com. It is inexpensive and contains the full gospel message for your consideration. This message is so important and extensive that it cannot adequately be contained in a few pages at the end of a book.

If you are a believer, you must go out into the world and seek peace through reconciliation as God did for us. These principles are to be lived and shared with others. You now have the tools to make your relationships last a lifetime. Go live them out and share them with others!

ABOUT THE AUTHOR

Dr. Donald Jones is currently a Christian Pastoral Counselor with thirty-eight years of experience in the fields of pastoral ministry, public education, and Christian counseling. He carries degrees and certificates from four major universities and from a variety of educational institutions. He has been a professor of Languages and Bible, a television commentator, and a featured speaker at a variety of events and seminars at churches, schools, and other organizations across the United States. He is a member in good standing of several secular and Christian professional organizations. Dr. Jones has been a published author since 1976. For further information view his website at www.donjonesphd.com.

* 9 7 8 1 9 4 6 3 6 8 0 4 1 *